r u s h

C O U N T E R P A R T S

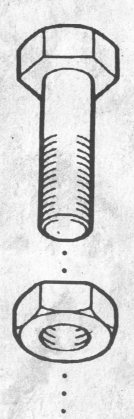

Art Direction, Illustration and Design by Hugh Syme
Photography by Andrew MacNaughtan
The Three Stooges ™ & © 1993 Norman Maurer Productions, Inc.

IME & TIDE CUT & DRIED
TRIED & TRUE FAST & LOOSE FREE
& CLEAR FAIR & SQUARE ROUGH & READY
SLOW & STEADY QUICK & DIRTY CHEAP & CHEERFUL NIP & TUCK TUCK &
ROLL DUCK & COVER DICK & JANE KICK & SCREAM CHOP & CHANGE BALL
& CHAIN SAFE & SOUND LOST & FOUND UP & AROUND BOW & SCRAPE
SHORT & SWEET AIM & FIRE LIVE & LEARN SLASH & BURN SMASH & GRAB
SEARCH & DESTROY FEAR & LOATHING BAIT & SWITCH CUT & PRINT RANK
& FILE WASH & WEAR CUT & PASTE LOUD & CLEAR UP & UP OUT & OUT SPIT
& POLISH SERVE & VOLLEY SEARCH & RESCUE CHALK & CHEESE RACK &
PINION HIT & RUN HIT & MISS HIGH & DRY HUE & CRY SKIN & BONES
STICKS & STONES STARS & STRIPES STRIPES & SOLIDS NEW & IMPROVED
DOLLARS & SENSE CHAPTER & VERSE OVER & OUT OUT & ABOUT ABOVE &
BEYOND FAR & AWAY HOPE & PRAY NIGHT & DAY SWING & SWAY DOWN &
AWAY HAPPY & GAY STRAIGHT & NARROW HIDE & SEEK HUNT & PECK
RHYME & REASON LOCK & KEY LUCY & RICKY MOOSE & SQUIRREL CATS &
DOGS TOOTH & NAIL HAND & FOOT HOOK & LADDER CLOAK & DAGGER
BLOCK & TACKLE BOW & ARROW ODDS & ENDS OFF & ON DEAD & GONE
HITHER & YON HEAVEN & HELL FIRE & BRIMESTONE FLOTSAM & JETSAM
FLORA & FAUNA MATTER & ENERGY MOMENTUM & INERTIA DRAWN &
QUARTERED TARRED & FEATHERED BOUND & GAGGED BOUND & DETER-
MINED THICK & THIN KITH & KIN BARBIE & KEN NOW & AGAIN PINS &
NEEDLES APPLES & ORANGES BELLS & WHISTLES CRUEL & UNUSUAL
CHARM & STRANGENESS ARMED & DANGEROUS WORDS & MUSIC GIN &
VERMOUTH RHYTHM & BLUES SOCKS & SHOES ROCK & ROLL SONG
& DANCE SMOKE & MIRRORS SHUCK & JIVE HOT & BOTHERED SUGAR &
SPICE COCK & BULL BECK & CALL BUMP & GRIND WINE & DINE RISE &
SHINE SLAP & TICKLE STAND & DELIVER LIFT & SEPARATE RIBBED &
LUBRICATED IN & OUT FORE & AFT GIVE & TAKE LONG & HARD OVER
& OVER KISS & TELL ALIVE & WELL STOP & GO HIGH & LOW YES & NO TOUCH &
GO FAST & SLOW BODY & SOUL FLESH & BLOOD ONE & ALL AMEN
PRIDE & JOY PEACE & LOVE TIME & AGAIN OVER & OVER

ANIMATE
Music by Lee and Lifeson/Lyrics by Peart

Polarize me
Sensitize me
Criticize me
Civilize me

Compensate me
Animate me
Complicate me
Elevate me

Goddess in my garden
Sister in my soul
Angel in my armor
Actress in my role

Daughter of a demon-lover
Empress of the hidden face
Priestess of the pagan mother
Ancient queen of inner space

Spirit in my psyche
Double in my role
Alter in my image
Struggle for control

Mistress of the dark unconscious
Mermaid of the lunar sea
Daughter of the great enchantress
Sister to the boy inside of me

My counterpart — my foolish heart
A man must learn to rule his tender part
A warming trend — a gentle friend
A man must build a fortress to defend

A secret face — a touch of grace
A man must learn to give a little space
A peaceful state — a submissive trait
A man must learn to gently dominate

STICK IT OUT
Music by Lee and Lifeson/Lyrics by Peart

Trust to your instinct
If it's safely restrained
Lightning reactions
Must be carefully trained

Heat of the moment
Curse of the young
Spit out your anger
Don't swallow your tongue

STICK IT OUT

Don't swallow the poison
SPIT IT OUT
Don't swallow your pride
STICK IT OUT
Don't swallow your anger
SPIT IT OUT
Don't swallow the lies

Natural reflex
Pendulum swing
You might be too dizzy
To do the right thing

Trial under fire
Ultimate proof
Moment of crisis
Don't swallow the truth

STICK IT OUT

Each time we bathe our reactions
In artificial light
Each time we alter the focus
To make the wrong move seem right

You get so used to deception
You make yourself a nervous wreck
You get so used to surrender
Running back to cover your neck

STICK IT OUT

CUT TO THE CHASE
Music by Lee and Lifeson/Lyrics by Peart

It is the fire that lights itself
But it burns with a restless flame
The arrow on a moving target
The archer must be sure of his aim
It is the engine that drives itself
But it chooses the uphill climb
A bearing on magnetic north
Growing farther away all the time

Can't stop — moving
Can't stop — moving
Can't stop —

YOU MAY BE RIGHT
IT'S ALL A WASTE OF TIME
I GUESS THAT'S JUST A CHANCE
I'M PREPARED TO TAKE
A DANGER I'M PREPARED TO FACE
CUT TO THE CHASE

It is the rocket that ignites itself
And launches its way to the stars
A driver on a busy freeway
Racing the oblivious cars

It's the motor of the western world
Spinning off to every extreme
Pure as a lover's desire
Evil as a murderer's dream

Young enough not to care too much
About the way things used to be
I'm young enough to remember the future —
The past has no claim on me

I'm old enough not to care too much
About what you think of me
But I'm young enough to remember the future
And the way things ought to be

WHAT KIND OF DIFFERENCE
CAN ONE PERSON MAKE?
CUT TO THE CHASE

NOBODY'S HERO
Music by Lee and Lifeson/Lyrics by Peart

I knew he was different, in his sexuality
I went to his parties, as the straight minority
It never seemed a threat to my masculinity
He only introduced me to a wider reality

As the years went by, we drifted apart
When I heard that he was gone
I felt a shadow cross my heart
But he's nobody's —

Hero — saves a drowning child
Cures a wasting disease
Hero — lands the crippled airplane
Solves great mysteries

Hero — not the handsome actor
Who plays a hero's role
Hero — not the glamor girl
Who'd love to sell her soul
If anybody's buying
NOBODY'S HERO

I didn't know the girl, but I knew her family
All their lives were shattered
in a nightmare of brutality
They try to carry on, try to bear the agony
Try to hold some faith
in the goodness of humanity

As the years went by, we drifted apart
When I heard that she was gone
I felt a shadow cross my heart
But she's nobody's—

Hero—the voice of reason
Against the howling mob
Hero—the pride of purpose
In the unrewarding job

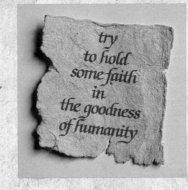

*try
to hold
some faith
in
the goodness
of humanity*

ahh yes to yes to ahh ahh to yes
why the sun why the sun

There is a fine line between love and illusion—
A fine place to penetrate
The gap between actor and act
The lens between wishes and fact

This is a fine place
To hesitate
Those bonfire lights in the lake of sky
The time between wonder and why

Some need to pray to the sun at high noon
Some need to howl at the midwinter moon
Reborn and baptized in a moment of grace
We just need a break—
From the headlong race

HOOK LINE SINKER LIGHTS CAMERA ACTION
CURLY LARRY MOE WIN PLACE SHOW TALL
DARK HANDSOME ANIMAL VEGETABLE MINERAL
SCISSORS PAPER STONE FLIP FLOP FLY
IFS ANDS BUTS HIGH WIDE HANDSOME TINKER
EVERS CHANCE LEFT RIGHT CENTER SHAKE RATTLE
ROLL SEX LIES VIDEOTAPE BENEATH BETWEEN BEHIND
FIRST LAST ALWAYS BAUBLES BANGLES BEADS HEALTHY
WEALTHY WISE DEAF DUMB BLIND ROBBIE CHIP ERNIE
PATTY MAXENE LAVERNE ATHOS PORTHOS ARAMIS
HOSS JOE & THE OTHER GUY LOCK STOCK BARREL TOM
DICK HARRY READY STEADY GO TIC TAC TOE GOOD
BAD UGLY THIS THAT THE OTHER LAND SEA SKY
ME MYSELF I FOLD SPINDLE MUTILATE HUEY DEWEY
LOUIE RUNS HITS ERRORS ATCHISON
TOPEKA SANTA FE FAITH HOPE CHARITY BEGINNING
MIDDLE END PAST PRESENT FUTURE WINE
WOMEN SONG MAN WOMAN CHILD
LUXE CALME VOLUPTÉ SCREWED BLUED TATTOOED
SONNY MICHAEL FREDO REGAN GONERIL CORDELIA
WINKEN BLINKEN NOD

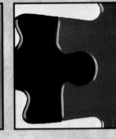

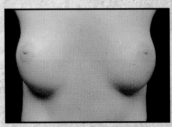

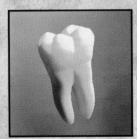

Hero—not the champion player
Who plays the perfect game
Not the glamor boy
Who loves to sell his name
Everybody's buying
NOBODY'S HERO

As the years went by, we drifted apart
When I heard that you were gone
I felt a shadow cross my heart

Hero

BETWEEN SUN AND MOON
Music by Lee and Lifeson/Lyrics by Peart & Dubois

There is a lake between sun and moon
Not too many know about
In the silence between whisper and shout
The space between wonder and doubt

This is a fine place
Shining face to face
Those bonfire lights in the mirror of sky
The space between wonder and why

ahh yes to yes to ahh ahh to yes
why the sun why the sun

*those bonfire
lights
in the
lake of
sky*

ALIEN SHORE
Music by Lee and Lifeson/Lyrics by Peart

You and I, we are strangers by one chromosome
Slave to the hormone, body and soul
In a struggle to be happy and free
Swimming in a primitive sea

You and I, we must dive below the surface
A world of red neon, and ultramarine
Shining bridges on the ocean floor
Reaching to the alien shore

For you and me — Sex is not a competition
For you and me — Sex is not a job description
For you and me — We agree

You and I, we are pressed into these solitudes
Color and culture, language and race

THE SPEED OF LOVE
Music by Lee and Lifeson/Lyrics by Peart

Love is born with lightning bolts
Electro-magnetic force
Burning skin and fireworks

At the speed of love
Nothing changes faster
Than the speed of love
My heart goes out to you

We don't have to talk
We don't even have to touch
I can feel your presence
In the silence that we share
Got to keep on moving
At the speed of love

Nothing changes faster
Than the speed of love
Got to keep on shining
At the speed of love
Nothing changes faster

Just variations on a theme
Islands in a much larger stream

For you and me — Race is not a competition
For you and me — Race is not a definition
For you and me — We agree
Reaching for the alien shore

You and I, we reject these narrow attitudes
We add to each other, like a coral reef
Building bridges on the ocean floor
Reaching for the alien shore

For you and me — We hold these truths to be self-evident
For you and me — We'd elect each other president
For you and me — We might agree
But that's just us

Reaching for the alien shore

A storm on a raging course

Like a force of nature,
Love can fade with the stars at dawn
Sometimes it takes all your strength
Just to keep holding on
At the speed of love
A radiance that travels
At the speed of love
My heart goes out to you

Love is born with solar flares
From two magnetic poles
It moves toward a higher plane
Where two halves make two wholes

Like a force of nature,
Love shines in many forms
One night we are bathed in light
One day carried away in storms

Than the speed of love
My heart goes out to you

DOUBLE AGENT
Music by Lee and Lifeson/Lyrics by Peart

Where would you rather be?
Anywhere but here
When will the time be right?
Anytime but now

On the edge of sleep,
I was drifting for half the night
Anxious and restless,
pressed down by the darkness
Bound up and wound up so tight
So many decisions, a million revisions
Caught between darkness and light...

Wilderness of mirrors
World of polished steel

My angels and my demons at war
Which one will lose—depends on what I choose
Or maybe which voice I ignore...

Wilderness of mirrors
Streets of cold desire
My precious sense of honor
Just a shield of rusty wire
I hold against the chaos—
And the cross of holy fire

Wilderness of mirrors
So easy to deceive
My precious sense of rightness
Is sometimes so naïve
So that which I imagine
Is that which I believe

COLD FIRE
Music by Lee and Lifeson/Lyrics by Peart

It was long after midnight
When we got to unconditional love
She said sure, my heart is boundless
But don't push my limits too far

I said if love is so transcendant
I don't understand these boundaries
She said just don't disappoint me—
You know how complex women are
I'll be around
If you don't let me down
Too far

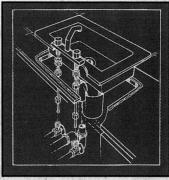

Gears and iron chains
Turn the grinding wheel
I run between the shadows
Some are phantoms, some are real

Where would you rather be?
Anywhere but here
When will the time be right?
Anytime but now
The doubt and the fear
I know would all disappear
Anywhere but here

On the edge of sleep,
I heard voices behind the door
The known and the nameless,
familiar and faceless

On the edge of sleep, I awoke to a sun so bright
Rested and fearless, cheered by your nearness
I knew which direction was right
The case had been tried by the jury inside
The choice between darkness and light...

It was just before sunrise
When we started on traditional roles
She said sure, I'll be your partner
But don't make too many demands

I said if love has these conditions
I don't understand those songs you love
She said this is not a love song
This isn't fantasy-land
I'll be around
If you don't push me down
Too far

Don't go too far —
The phosphorescent wave on a tropical sea
Is a cold fire
Don't cross the line —
The pattern of moonlight on the bedroom floor
Is a cold fire
Don't let me down —
The flame at the heart of a pawnbroker's diamond
Is a cold fire
Don't break the spell —
The look in your eyes as you head for the door
Is a cold fire

Love is blind if you are gentle
Love can turn to a long, cold burn

EVERYDAY GLORY
Music by Lee and Lifeson/Lyrics by Peart

In the house where nobody laughs
And nobody sleeps
In the house where love lies dying
And the shadows creep
A little girl hides, shaking,
With her hands on her ears
Pushing back the tears, 'til the pain disappears

Mama says some ugly words
Daddy pounds the wall
They can fight about their little girl later
But right now, they don't care at all

Just one spark of decency
Against the starless night
One glow of hope and dignity
A child can follow the light
No matter what they say
No matter what they say . . .

If the future's looking dark
We're the ones who have to shine
If there's no one in control
We're the ones who draw the line
Though we live in trying times —
We're the ones who have to try
Though we know that time has wings —
We're the ones who have to fly

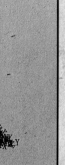

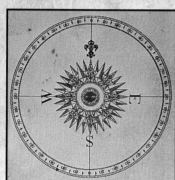

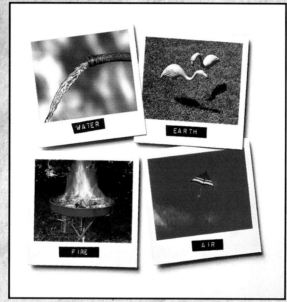

No matter what they say . . .
No matter what they say . . .

EVERYDAY PEOPLE
EVERYDAY SHAME
EVERYDAY PROMISE
SHOT DOWN IN FLAMES

EVERYDAY SUNRISE
ANOTHER EVERYDAY STORY
RISE FROM THE ASHES —
A BLAZE OF EVERYDAY GLORY

In the city where nobody smiles
And nobody dreams
In the city where desperation
Drives the bored to extremes

CONTENTS

ANIMATE

Lyrics by
NEIL PEART

Music by
GEDDY LEE and ALEX LIFESON

Daugh - ter of___ a de - mon lov - er,
Mis - tress of___ the dark un - con - scious,

em - press of the hid - den face.
mer - maid of the lu - nar sea.

Priest - ess of the pa - gan moth - er,
Daugh - ter of the great___ en - chant - ress,

an - cient queen of in -
sis - ter to the boy

ner space._____
in - side of me.

STICK IT OUT

Lyrics by
NEIL PEART

Music by
GEDDY LEE and ALEX LIFESON

Moderately fast

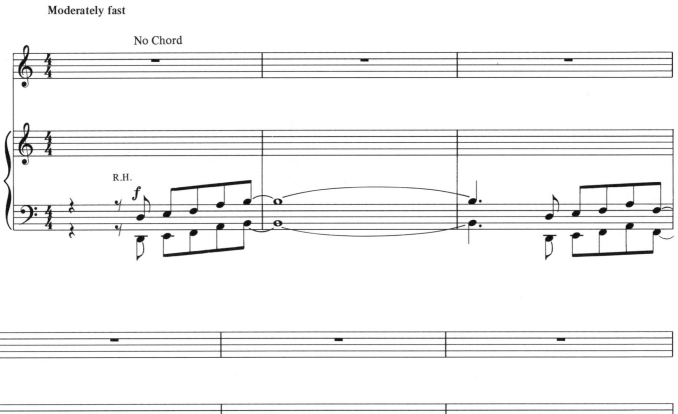

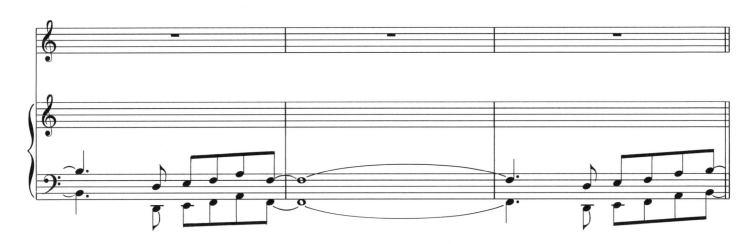

Spit out your an - ger,   don't swal - low your tongue.__
Mo - ment of cri - sis,   don't swal - low the truth.__

Stick it out.__   Don't swal - low the poi - son.__

Spit it out.__   Don't swal - low your pride.__   Stick it out.__   Don't

swal - low your an - ger.___ Spit it out.___ Don't swal - low the lies.___

swal - low the lies.___

Stick it out.___

CUT TO THE CHASE

Lyrics by
NEIL PEART

Music by
GEDDY LEE and ALEX LIFESON

It is the fire_____ that lights_____ it - self
et that ig - nites it - self

but it burns_____ with a rest - less flame.
and launch - es it's way_____ to the stars.

The
A

ar - row on a mov - ing tar - get;
driv - er on a bus - y free - way,

the arch - er must be sure_____ of his aim.
rac - ing the ob - liv - i - ous cars.

NOBODY'S HERO

Lyrics by
NEIL PEART

Music by
GEDDY LEE and ALEX LIFESON

He - ro, not the hand - some ac - tor who
He - ro, not the cham - pion play - er who

plays_____ a he - ro's role.
plays_____ the per - fect game.

He - ro, not the glam - or girl_____ who'd
He - ro, not the glam - or boy_____ who

love to sell her_____ soul._____ If
loves to sell his_____ name._____

BETWEEN SUN AND MOON

Lyrics by
NEIL PEART and PYE DuBOIS

Music by
GEDDY LEE and ALEX LIFESON

Moderate Rock

Some need to

Ahh___ yes   to yes___   to ahh___   ahh___

ALIEN SHORE

Lyrics by
NEIL PEART

Music by
GEDDY LEE and ALEX LIFESON

Moderate Rock

Reach - ing— for the al - i - en shore._____

THE SPEED OF LOVE

Lyrics by
NEIL PEART

Music by
GEDDY LEE and ALEX LIFESON

We don't have to talk, We don't ev-

en have to touch. I can feel___ your pres - ence

in the si - lence that we___ share.___ Got to

DOUBLE AGENT

Lyrics by
NEIL PEART

Music by
GEDDY LEE and ALEX LIFESON

Moderate rock

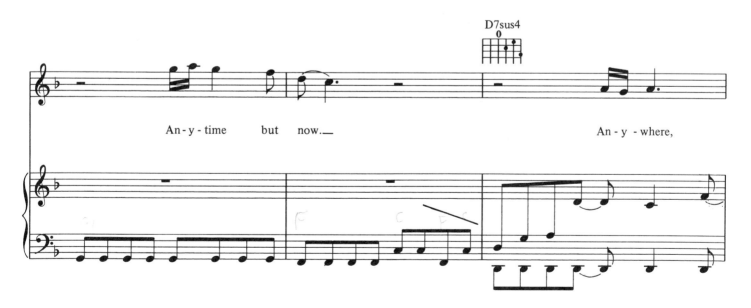

an - y - where but here.

An - y - where,   an - y - where but here.

where but here, _____ an - y - where but here. _____

Guitar solo (ad lib)

LEAVE THAT THING ALONE!

Music by
GEDDY LEE and ALEX LIFESON

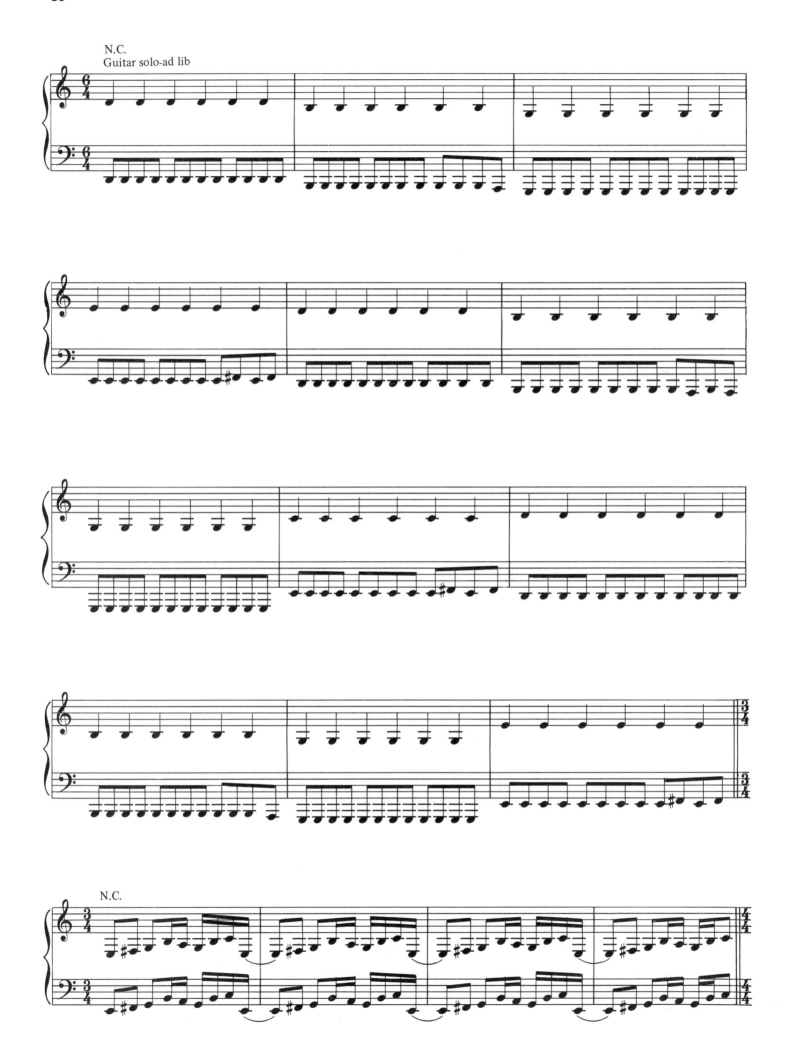

COLD FIRE

Lyrics by
NEIL PEART

Music by
GEDDY LEE and ALEX LIFESON

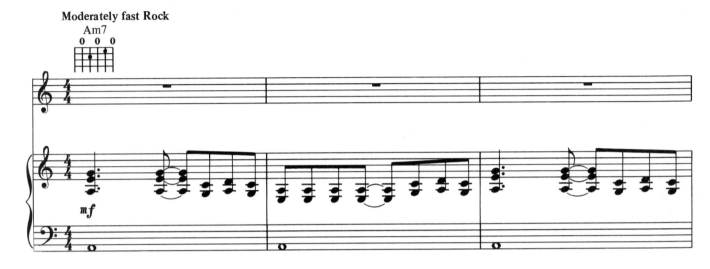

but don't make too man - y___ de - mands.___

I said if love___ has these___ con - di - tions, I don't un-

der - stand___ those songs you love.___ She said, this is not___ a love___

___ song, this is - n't fan - tas - y___ land.

(Don't go to far.___)

EVERYDAY GLORY

Lyrics by
NEIL PEART

Music by
GEDDY LEE and ALEX LIFESON

In the house where no - bod - y laughs and no - bod - y sleeps,

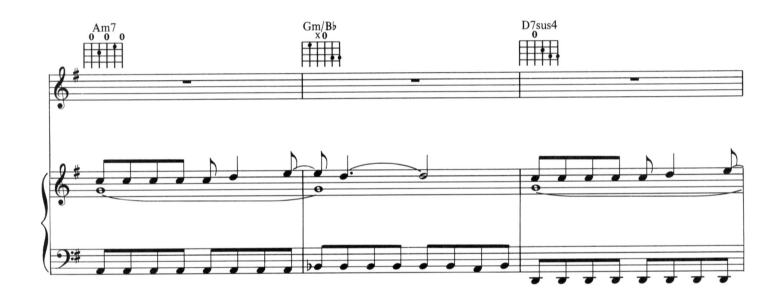

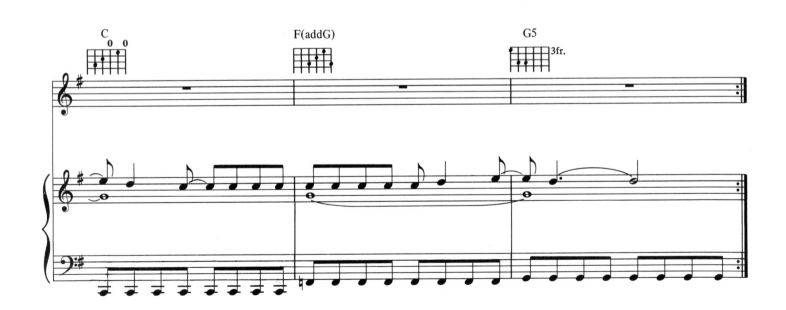